YOU ARE ABOUT TO READ MATERIAL THAT IS EXCERPTED FROM A NEW BOOK EXPLAINING HOW MONEY CAN WORK FOR *YOU*; HOW *YOU* CAN BECOME FINANCIALLY INDEPENDENT.

National best seller *The Power of MONEY DYNAMICS* by Venita Van Caspel has won wide acclaim by both financial investors and advisors and the public. It tells how to win life's biggest game—the money game. And no one is better qualified to tell you how to win than Venita Van Caspel. She is the nation's first lady of financial planning being the first woman member of the Pacific Stock Exchange, president of the Houston stockbrokerage firm of Van Caspel and Company, Inc., and president of Van Caspel Planning Services. In her book, *The Power of Money Dynamics*, Mrs. Van Caspel draws on her vast financial experience to show *you*—not the professional money manager, the government, or the insurance agent—but *you*, the individual, how to make money work. You'll find chapters full of sound professional tips on building financial independence, inflation, loaning your money, stocks, mutual funds, real estate investment, life insurance, self-employment, financing a college education or a house, taxes—just everything you need to know to win the money game.

After reading this booklet, you'll want to order a copy of *The Power of Money Dynamics*. Please use the order coupon on the following page.

©1983 by RESTON PUBLISHING COMPANY, INC., Reston, Virginia
A Prentice-Hall Company

NOW! YOU CAN BUILD FINANCIAL INDEPENDENCE WITH THE STEP-BY-STEP GUIDE TO EFFECTIVE MONEY MANAGEMENT.

Send to:
RESTON PUBLISHING COMPANY, INC.
11480 Sunset Hills Road
Reston, Virginia 22090

or call: 800-336-0338

The author: Venita Van Caspel, President of the stock brokerage firm, Van Caspel & Co., Inc., and owner of Van Caspel Planning Services.

YES! Please send me this new best selling money management guidebook. When I see how Venita Van Caspel's easy-to-follow advice on successful investing can help me to win financial security, I'll send $20.00 for each book plus $2.93 postage and handling for the first copy, 45¢ postage for each additional copy plus my state's sales tax.

SAVE! If payment plus your state's sales tax accompanies order, publisher pays postage and handling!

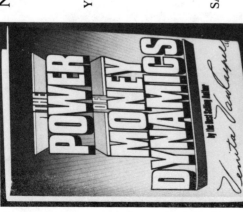

R5570-8

Please send me 1 copy.　　Please send me 2 copies.　　Please send me 3 copies.

NAME _____

STREET _____

CITY _____ STATE _____ ZIP _____

PHONE _____

V-0726-B1(6)

PREFACE

You are living in an era of tremendous change! Dynamic, challenging, and frustrating change is taking place in family relationships, international affairs, living styles, technology, and especially in the nurture and investment of your money. To win the money game in this decade— and win you must—you will have to develop a special kind of expertise, mental attitude, agility, diversity, and determination.

It will not be change, but rather your reaction to change, that will determine your financial future. Change can greatly enhance your fortune, or it can destroy it; make you a millionaire or a pauper; delight you or disappoint you; exhilarate you or depress you. Change brings with it heightened potential and devastating crevices of danger.

How you cope with this inevitable change will determine whether you'll win or lose the vital money game. The money game is not like any other game. You cannot choose whether you'll play, for the money game is the only game in town. Since you have no choice but to play, it behooves you to learn to play the game very well, for losing could mean spending your life in a state of frustrating, devastating financial insecurity.

Financial independence can be yours if you have an average ability to earn and a little discipline to save, if you apply the information you'll learn in this book, and if you are granted enough time. You have control over the first three variables.

There is probably nothing that you'll ever learn to do that will become as easy and as exhilarating as making money once you've mastered the rules. You'll find that there will be an investment for every season, but there will be no investment for all seasons. Agility and diversification will become your keystones as you learn from this book how to take advantage of the dynamics of the Economic Recovery Tax Act of 1981 (ERTA) and how to position your assets effectively where demand is greater than supply in order to compound your money rapidly.

This is a personal book. Financial planning must of necessity be personal, for you are different from any other person. You are a unique creation and have developed in your own unique way. You have different financial objectives, assets, tax bracket, temperament, emotions, and time schedules than even your closest friend. Your financial program, therefore, must be designed for you and for you alone.

If you and I could sit down and plan your financial future, I would ask you many pertinent questions about you and your money. I would then endeavor to design a program that fits not only your financial needs, but your emotional needs as well. Designing a program for your financial needs is relatively simple, once I know all the facts; but mapping a course that fits your temperament and your prejudices and then communicating these ideas to you in such a way that you will understand and then act upon them is a continuous challenge.

Since you and I may never have the opportunity to sit and discuss your financial plans, I have designed this book to give you a step-by-step guide to use in designing your own financial blueprint and keeping it updated constantly to fit these dynamic times.

I will be sharing with you the knowledge I have acquired over the past twenty years as a Certified Financial Planner. During that time it has been my joy to watch the assets of my clients grow and to see their dimension for living expand through the application of the money and living skills that I have taught them and helped them to apply. Added to these people I have helped personally have been the vast numbers who have read my last three books: *Money Dynamics, The New Money Dynamics,* and *Money Dynamics for the 1980s.* My daily mail enthusiastically detailing successful results is an avalanche of joy to me, for nothing delights me more than receiving testimonials of success from my readers and valued clients.

It continues to be my privilege to be in daily contact with some of our nation's top policymakers, the most expert observers of the money scene, our leading financial planners, and a large number of successful business and professional people who make decisions that affect us all.

From this vast exposure to information, my training, and my years of experience, I have developed a certain expertise.

Through my seminars, speeches, books, and counseling, I feel that I have helped raise the level of financial independence of my fellow Texans, and through the enormous sale and use of my past three books, the financial independence of a nation. Financial Planners, stockbrokers, and enthusiastic readers across the nation continue to recommend to their clients and friends my books, my national Public Broadcast Television series ("The Moneymakers," carried by 182 stations nationwide), and my national *Money Dynamics Letter*. These are helping Americans learn how to profit from owning a part of American industry, real estate, energy, and a vast number of other areas of our free enterprise system. Such ownership is vitally important, for if they do not own and participate in the fruits of the system, Americans will vote to destroy it, resulting in one of the world's greatest tragedies. We know that the free enterprise system is not perfect, but it is the best system yet devised. It has brought the greatest good to the greatest number of people.

Now, reach out your hands and let me grasp them firmly as I lead you down the road toward financial independence. To provide you with a solid foundation it will be necessary at the beginning of this book to introduce you to some tables that may not be as exciting as we would both like for them to be. But do persevere, devour them, and let them seep deeply into your subconscious mind. You'll find them invaluable in the attainment of your predetermined worthwhile goal. Now, let's begin our exciting journey together toward your financial independence.

TO WIN THE MONEY GAME

Welcome to the exciting world of money and its marvelous kaleidoscope of change—changes that will force your old strategies into obsolescence and bring you new opportunities in abundance!

Don't be discouraged if you are discovering that all the old money rules your parents taught you aren't working, for there are many more productive ways to put your money to work today. You can now own the thing that owns the thing. You can see a need and fill it. You can be an owner of a vast combination of productive assets and participate in their growth while sheltering a large portion of this growth and the income it produces from the devastation of taxation.

You are truly fortunate to be living in this exciting period of investment history. In my many years as a Certified Financial Planner I have never seen so many viable investment opportunities for both large and small investors.

The application of the techniques clearly defined in this book will make the next ten years the most profitable you've ever experienced.

Money Has No Gender

Throughout this book I will use the masculine pronoun in a neutral way to mean "he or she." I have found that God has been very fair in His apportionment of brains. He has made women as intelligent and as capable as men, so in this book I'll not bother myself with all this "he-she" business, but rather will devote myself to the order of the day: helping you make your money work effectively for you.

The same money rules apply to women as to men. If you are a woman, don't ever think it is your inalienable right that a man should take care of your financial security. The single state—whether it is through choice, circumstances, death, or divorce—will probably be your lot for at least a part or all of your life. Even if you marry, you have an obligation to be a financial partner to your husband and to be as well informed as you can about money. I have found that love is not so much looking into each other's eyes, but looking in the same direction—and the same is certainly true when it comes to money.

In the past, too many women have been taught "It's not nice to talk about money." You'd better believe it is nice to talk about money—and to learn about money—or you won't have any. The sweet damsel who sits around waiting for Prince Charming to come riding into her life on the proverbial white horse and take care of all her financial needs may very well find herself cleaning up after his steed.

Dear Investor

My greeting to you is "Dear Investor" because you are an investor. You are either investing all of your wealth in today's goods and services or you are reserving a portion of it to invest in tomorrow's goods and services. You do not have the choice of whether you will invest, but you do have the choice of how you will invest. The wisdom you bring to bear on these choices will have a greater influence on your financial future than the amount of money that comes your way.

Do you want to consume all that you earn today and hope that somehow tomorrow will take care of itself? As short-sighted as this may seem, it is the course being taken by the vast majority of your fellow citizens.

Three Sources of Income

If you'll stand back and objectively analyze your potential sources of future income, you will find that there are three chief sources.

The first is you at work. However, there will come a time when, regardless of how badly you want to work, the world will not let you. It will retire you.

The second source is your money at work. If you make proper preparation and turn some of your income into growing investments, a time will come when you will no longer have to work for your money, but you will be able to trade places with your money and let your money work for you. I have found that income from capital is immensely more secure than income from labor.

The third source of income is charity.

Man at work, money at work, charity—which source do you want to depend on when you retire? Since "man at work" may not be an option open to you and "charity" has rarely brought happiness, apply your intelligence toward assuring yourself that there is sufficient "money at work" to retire in financial dignity.

Why do so many fail to become financially independent? During my years as a financial planner I have searched for the answers, for I have been convinced that if I could discover these answers, I could help thousands of people avoid living twenty to thirty years of their lives in the tragic state of financial insecurity and enable them to retire in financial dignity.

Six Reasons So Many Fail

I believe I have found the reasons. There are six, and here they are: (1) procrastination; (2) failure to establish a definite financial goal; (3) ignorance of what money must do to accomplish that goal; (4) failure to understand and apply our tax laws; (5) being sold the wrong kind of life insurance; and (6) failure to develop a winning mental attitude about money. When you have completed reading this book, you will know how to avoid all these reasons for failure and you will have a definite blueprint for financial success.

Procrastination

Procrastination can be the greatest deterrent to reaching your goal of financial independence. Time can be your greatest ally. If you have a sufficient amount of time, you will not need as much money to put to work. The less time you have, the more money it will take. Do not waste this precious commodity—a commodity that is distributed to each of us equally.

Procrastination is a deadly enemy of your obligation to retire in financial dignity. Sometimes you may confuse goals and obligations. A larger home, a boat, travel to foreign lands—all of these can be your goals. But preparing to retire in financial dignity is more than a goal. It is your obligation, a debt that you owe yourself and others—your family, your community, and other taxpayers. With proper financial planning and sound money management, it is a debt that you can pay, so as to make your retirement years happy instead of haphazard, comfortable instead of dependent.

I have observed that in the early years of life, when spending habits are formed, thoughts of retirement are far away and have little relationship to current needs and even less to future needs. The habit becomes reinforced with the same passing of time that brings retirement closer. Then when retirement time is so near as to be of immediate concern, it is often too late to make adequate preparation.

Procrastination often stands in the shadows, awaiting its opportunity to spoil your chance for success. You may even be procrastinating because you fear success. You will probably go through life as a failure if you wait for the "time to be right" to start doing something worthwhile. Do not wait. The time will never be "just right" to start your journey down the road to financial independence. Life is a journey, not a destination. Take all your "someday I'll do it" ideas and put them to work now. There is no such thing as a future decision. There are only present decisions that affect the future.

Make "Do It Now" your slogan for the rest of your life! And, always aim high. If you aim for the stars, you certainly should not end up with a handful of mud.

Failure to Establish a Goal

The second reason that many fail to become financially independent is that they fail to establish a goal. If you aim at nothing in life, you are liable to hit nothing. I've never had anyone come to me and say, "Venita, I plan to fail." Yet I've observed many who failed to plan and who unfortunately met with the same dismal results.

After moderating "Successful Texans" and "The Moneymakers" and after listening to the life stories of the other recipients who were honored, as I was, with the Horatio Alger Award for Distinguished Americans—and who have attained success under our free enterprise system—I have reached some conclusions about the necessary ingredients for success in life and in money matters. Successful people differ in appearance, voice, height, weight, education, and family background, but they all have one thing in common: they know where they are going. Each has a goal. If anything sidetracks one of them, or if something doesn't work the way they planned, they just dust themselves off and go right back in the direction of their goal. After many years of observation, I am in complete agreement with the famous psychologist William James, who said, "Anything the mind can believe and conceive, it can achieve."

Visualize your financial goal right now. Your mind will not let you conceive what you cannot achieve. Write out your immediate, intermediate, and distant goals in a clear and concise manner, stating exactly what your goals are and your timetable for accomplishing each of them. This will crystallize your dreams and cause you to develop a different life-style in which more power and energy are devoted to each day's activities. You will become a different person. Problems will be looked upon in a different light and you will find you can focus on the solution. A by-product of goal setting will be determination. It is already a force inside of you and goal setting releases the power of determination so that it can propel you to financial levels that were heretofore beyond your reach.

Success in money management is not a will-o'-the-wisp that comes to some and not to others because of fate, chance, or luck. Success in money management can be predicted, if you have a plan and if you follow that plan.

If you give a blueprint to a skillful builder, do you think that it will be a matter of chance, or luck, that he will complete the structure successfully? Of course not. He merely begins at the beginning and follows the plan step by step to its completion.

This book is your blueprint for success. If you follow it, financial independence will be yours.

Ignorance about Money

A third reason for failing is ignorance of what money must do to accomplish a financial goal.

There is an educational void in our nation. We are raising a generation of financial illiterates. Even our college graduates cannot figure simple percentages.

The tragic mistakes they are making because of these deficiencies in our system are destroying their dreams, their hopes, their families, and their pride in themselves and their country. Their hoped-for rewards from their talents and skills are disappearing like vapor. From my years as a stockbroker and later a certified financial planner, I have observed daily the devastating effect of this void.

Our schools are doing a tremendous job of teaching the know-how of a vocation. They are offering their students a vast array of

opportunities to prepare themselves for the career of their choice, from basic mechanics to electronics. They are offering them the opportunity to acquire knowledge in a wide variety of fields such as engineering, chemistry, computer technology, sales, distribution, management, and accounting. They are also offering students courses that will prepare them to live enriched lives through the study of music and the various arts.

Yet our schools are not teaching students the one subject that they will need to live well in our free enterprise system—and that is how to manage their money. This vacuum is so great that the average couple cannot begin to defend themselves against the financial uncertainties and multitude of choices they face in our complex society.

This lack of financial know-how is not only destroying the American dream, but can lead these financially illiterate citizens to vote to destroy our free enterprise system. Any person will be against something that he does not understand or that he feels he cannot participate in. The destruction of this system would be one of the greatest tragedies to beset our world.

The free enterprise system is not perfect by any stretch of the imagination, but it is the best system yet devised for bringing the greatest good to the greatest number of people.

I find that people are frightened today. All the old money rules are not working. For the first time, they have taken their money out of the bank and they probably won't put it back. They've put it in money market mutual funds (which I'll discuss later), but this is a temporary home and they will need to search for more rewarding investments to survive.

Failure to Learn our Tax Laws

The fourth reason many fail to achieve financial independence is that they fail to learn and apply our tax laws. The only money you'll ever get to spend at the grocery store is what the government lets you keep. Every investment you make must be carefully correlated with your tax bracket or you are making the wrong investment. You must learn to avoid taxes—not evade them. Learn to defer taxes, convert to classifications where the taxes are lower, and learn to think in terms of tax equivalents. Throughout this book you'll find how to invest for "keepable" income.

Contrary to any misleading headlines you may read, your total tax bill will not be cut appreciably in the decade of the 1980s. Even with the so-called tax cut provided by the Economic Recovery Tax Act of 1981, tax-bracket creep and the added Social Security taxes will probably make your total tax bill higher than it was before the cut and the purchasing power of what is left lower. The massive tax increase in the guise of a mislabeled "windfall-profits tax" (on which there can be and often is a tax without a profit) is really a sales tax on gasoline, heating oil, and other petroleum products. It was called "windfall profits" to deceive a public ignorant of basic economics.

The real burden of taxes is what the government spends. If the government spends more than it takes in, you and I pay the difference in the form of inflation and the interest expense on the national debt.

The Economic Recovery Act of 1981

ERTA, as it has come to be called, was designed by its originators to facilitate the reindustrialization of the United States and to increase personal savings. Our congressional process greatly dulled its effectiveness by making the cuts in taxes come too slowly to accomplish the maximum good. Now we must wait to see whether Congress and the American public will give the changes time to heal the damages caused by many years of excessive government spending and costly red tape combined with punitive disincentive tax laws for individuals and business. As a nation, we've come to expect instant solutions—the quick fix. After all, every night on television we solve major problems in an hour, with six breaks for the good life.

On October 2, 1981, I was a guest on a television show and the host said to me, "Well, Reaganomics certainly isn't working is it?" My answer to him was, "The program only became effective yesterday. Don't you think we should give it more than twenty-four hours before we pass judgment?" Thirty years of moving away from productivity and the incentives to be productive cannot be changed in a few hours or a few years. But in time, the direction can be changed through productive investments in plants and equipment and through the reduction of unwise increases in federal spending and the money supply. These measures could move us toward a balanced budget, wages that reflect productivity, and a lowering of interest rates, which in turn should allow our industries to produce products that can compete nationally and abroad.

If you have not read the highlights of ERTA, do so now. My favorite reference book is *Research Institute Master Federal Tax Manual* (it can be obtained by writing to the address in the Appendix). It is written in lay language. How can you play the money and tax game if you don't know the rules? No better than you can play any other game. You are playing the very serious game of financial power and survival, and this book will teach you how to win.

The Wrong Kind of Life Insurance

The fifth reason that people fail to become financially independent is that they have been sold the wrong kind of life insurance. I say "sold" because if they had received sufficient information about the purpose of life insurance and how each policy was put together, they would not have made the tragic mistakes that they have made.

My publisher excerpted and made available for distribution Chapter 13, "Life Insurance—The Great National Consumer Fraud," from my two previous books. Over 2 million copies are now in circulation across the United States. I am delighted with the fantastic impact this chapter has made and is continuing to make on the whole insurance industry, and the number of families that will have a better opportunity to achieve financial independence because they have followed my instructions. I have changed the title of this chapter slightly for this book because those who profit so handsomely from selling the wrong kind of insurance have been able to get it banned or its use curtailed in eight states. It is my hope that the change from "fraud" to "dilemma" will somewhat reduce their success and make it possible for more families to benefit from the information it contains. You'll learn what you need to know about life insurance when you read Chapter 13 of this book.

Failure to Develop a Winning Mentality

The sixth reason that people fail to win the money game is that they fail to develop a winning mentality. The demarcation line between success and failure is often very narrow and can be crossed if the desire can be stimulated, if competent guidance can be made available, and if sufficient encouragement and incentive are provided.

There are many vital parts to the psychology of winning. Some of the most important for financial independence are attitude, effort, lack of prejudice, persistence and enthusiasm.

Attitude. There is a truly magic word that you should place not only in your vocabulary, but also in the very fiber of your being if you desire to be successful in the realm of money or in any other important area of your life. That magic word is ATTITUDE!

Everything in life operates according to the law of cause and effect. You must produce the causes; the rewards will take care of themselves. A good attitude leads to good results; a fair attitude, to fair results; a bad attitude, to bad results.

You will shape your own financial life by the attitudes that you hold each day. If you have a poor attitude toward learning about money management, you will not learn very much until you change your attitude. If you have an attitude of failure, you are defeated before you start.

Sometimes a prospective client will say, "If I invest, the market will go down. I've never made any money in the market." Until he can change his attitude, he will not become a successful investor. I have found that truly prepared, working optimists always make money. I have also found that pessimists rarely do.

Look around you. Study successful people. You'll find that they go sailing through life from one success to another. These people have the attitude that they can accomplish whatever they set out to do. Because of this attitude, they do accomplish their goals. They achieve some remarkable things and the world calls them successful, brilliant, lucky, and so on.

Luck. As you may guess, I do not believe in luck. Luck happens when preparedness and opportunity get together. If you are prepared, you will be lucky. A close friend of mine, who is a well-known and respected business consultant, studied a particular company and bought shares of stock while it was still in its infancy. These shares have now grown in value tremendously and have made him a very wealthy man. There are those who would scoff and say, "I should be so lucky." It wasn't just luck. He was prepared.

When he and his wife were first married, they scrimped and saved and lived in a modest apartment. They even sold their car and rode the bus to work so they could save a nest egg. It was this nest egg, which they had so painfully saved, that was used to make their "lucky" investment. Had they not prepared, they would not have had the means of availing themselves of all this "luck."

Prejudice. We all have prejudices, but we should continually work to rid ourselves of them. In counseling, I sometimes encounter a couple who seem to be saying to me, "Please don't confuse us with facts." They do not want to know the truth. The truth will not make them free, regardless of how carefully or intelligently it may be presented to them.

Lack of Concentrated Efforts. To become a good investor, you must seriously apply your intelligence, use your ability to acquire knowledge, and give your attention to details and timing. If you cannot, will not, or do not have the ability to do these things successfully for yourself, do not take a distorted ego trip by not admitting that someone may be able to do something better than you can do it. Put the professionals to work for you.

Desiring Something for Nothing. If I were to distill all the wisdom I've ever learned into nine words, they would be: There is no such thing as a free lunch. I have observed two drives where this is evident. One is the gambling instinct, which has driven many to failure in the market. Investing, properly approached with constant supervision, is in my opinion the safest long-term thing that can be done with money. Speculation, on the other hand, can be risky. This desire for a "free lunch" is often seen working in the opposite manner by those who will leave their funds in a savings institution because they refuse to pay a brokerage commission to get their funds invested. The money that they "save" is often very costly.

In making an investment decision, the important factor is not what it "costs." You do not care what it costs, but you are truly concerned with what it pays.

Lack of Enthusiasm. I do believe I can forgive almost any shortcoming a person may have except lack of enthusiasm; and it is especially essential in the acquisition of money. Enthusiasm is contagious; if you have it in sufficient quantities, others will welcome you into their group. You will be more in touch with the needs and thinking of the people around you, and you can profit from the investment opportunities that will become obvious to you.

Guessing Instead of Thinking. Information is available about almost any subject you need. Don't let indifference or plain laziness keep you from acquiring the facts essential to making good judgments. Acquire the major points of information you need—you'll never have "all" the information. If you wait that long, you'll probably make your decision too late for maximum profit. I find that most decisions are made too late rather than too soon. We all have a tendency to have a good laugh when someone says, "Do something, even if it's wrong." I have found that there is usually more merit in this than is apparent on first blush. As Ralph Waldo Emerson said, "Do the thing and you will have the power."

Lack of Capital. Build up your nest egg, and do it while you are young. Remember to pay yourself first and then don't spend the nest egg, but use it as collateral for levering a larger egg and then a larger one. Never consider any earnings on your investments as spendable until you have reached your goal of financial independence. This is how you develop your money power. Your banker will welcome you with open arms if you have collateral to back your bankable idea.

Being Overinfluenced by the Opinions of Others. I have observed that those who fail to accumulate sufficient amounts of money are easily influenced by the opinions of other people. Opinions are cheap. You will find them everywhere. There are always those who are just waiting to foist their opinions on you if you will accept them. If you let others overinfluence you when you are reaching decisions about your money, you will not succeed.

Lack of Persistence. Are you a good "starter" and a poor "finisher," as so many are? Each year we must close our reservations early for our January financial planning seminars because we cannot seat all those who want to come. This year our overflow seminar in addition to our regular three-session seminar had 700 people in it.

If you begin a financial planning program and happen to experience a temporary setback, do not give up. I've observed this at times when a client starts a monthly investment program. If the market goes up after he starts his program, he'll happily put in his investment each month, but if the market goes down, he'll abandon the program, regardless of how I've tried to explain that dollar-cost-averaging results can benefit from stock market fluctuations. There is no substitute for persistence. If you make persistence your watchword, you'll discover that "old man failure" will finally become weary of you and will make his exit. Failure cannot cope with persistence.

During my twenty years as a financial planner, I've searched for the common denominator of success. I've noticed that one particular characteristic seems to run through each life—the successful person has formed the habit of doing the things that failures do not like to do.

Perhaps you think that you have certain dislikes that are peculiar to you, and that successful people don't have these dislikes but like to do the very things that you don't like to do. This isn't true. They don't like to do them any more than you do. These successful people are doing these very things they don't like to do in order to accomplish the things they want to accomplish. Successful people are motivated by the desire for pleasing results. Failures search for pleasing experiences and are satisfied with results that can be obtained by doing things they like to do.

Inability to Make a Decision. I have found over and over again that those who succeed in making large sums of money reach decisions promptly and change them, if at all, very slowly. I have also found that those who fail to make money reach decisions very slowly, if at all, and change them frequently and quickly. Procrastination and indecision are twins. Pluck this grim pair out of your life before they bind you to the treadmill of financial failure.

Yesterday is past, tomorrow is only a promise. Only today is legal tender. Only this moment of time is yours. Where you will be financially next year or ten years from now will depend on the decision that you make today—or the ones you don't make.

Of the many studies of successful people, near the top of the list of characteristics is their ability to be decisive. Of the many studies of failures, at the top of the list of reasons for their failure is procrastination. Study, think, plan, act!

Making a Decision is a Privilege. No one can make your decisions for you. You will find that free advice about your money is always available. It's usually those who lean back and give you the most "positive" advice whose finances are bordering on catastrophe. They are often wrong, but never in doubt.

There have been times when I, or one of our team of financial planners, has counseled a couple who have attended all three sessions of our investment seminar and thus have listened to me for at least five hours. They have asked for an appointment, and one of us has spent two hours with them in uninterrupted personal conference. When it comes time to apply this information to their own personal finances, they will say, "This sounds fine, but let us go home and think it over." On the surface this sounds like a prudent, sensible thing to do, doesn't it? However, I find that it usually is not. They already have all the information they need. They will not be "thinking it over" after they leave. Dozens of other matters will require their attention. They are trying to avoid making a decision, not realizing that no decision is a decision. They are deciding that where their money is now is the best place for it to be—for that is the result brought about by their lack of action. Always remember, indecision is decision—usually against you.

Overcaution. The person who takes no chances generally must take whatever is left over after others have finished choosing. Overcaution is as bad, if not worse, than lack of caution. Both should be avoided. Life will always contain an element of chance. Not to win is not a sin. But not to try is a tragedy.

There is no reward without risk. If you've never missed when investing, you've not been in there trying, or you've been holding your losers far too long for maximum profits. Play the money game well, but never safely. Avoid a life of no hits, no runs, no errors!

The reason many are not successful investors is that they are afraid to do anything with their money, so they leave it in the bank or savings and loan for years, where inflation destroys it. That's not playing it safe. That's playing it dumb.

Lack of Self-Discipline. Another cause of failure is lack of self-discipline. The secret of financial independence is not brilliance or luck, but the discipline to save a part of all you earn and to put it to work in shares of industry, real estate, natural resources, tangible assets, and so on.

To be a winner, you must practice self-discipline. Self-discipline achieves goals. There are those who think of self-discipline as "doing without." To me, it is "doing within." It's a mental and physical process. It's your own vivid visualization of financial independence. Winners are those who are doing within while they are doing without.

Expectations. The successful people with whom I have visited seem to find their accomplishments not too difficult and often surprisingly easy, simply because it seems so few are really trying.

Winners look at life as a game—one they expect to win, are prepared to win, desire to win, and know how to win. They have conscientiously nurtured and developed the habit of winning. They affirm and reaffirm to themselves each day that they are self-determined.

Acquire Equity. Again, I emphasize, own the thing that owns the thing! Own the assets that create the wealth. If you are, or remain a lender, you will receive only the crumbs and the owners will be the winners. This book will teach you how to be an owner.

Money. Rid yourself of the old myth, if it has been plaguing you, that money is not important. It is important—vitally important! It is just as important as the food it buys, the shelter it provides, the doctor bills it pays, and the education it helps to procure. Money is important to you as you live in a civilized society. To split hairs and say that it is not as important as other things is just arguing for the sake of the exercise. Nothing will take the place of money in areas in which money works.

What is money? Money is the harvest of your production. The amount of money you will receive will always be in direct ratio to the need for what you do, your ability to do it, and the difficulty of replacing you.

I'm amazed at the number of people who tell me that they want money but don't want to take the time and trouble to qualify for it. Until they qualify for it, there's no way they can earn it.

All you need is a plan—a road map—and the courage to arrive at your destination, knowing in advance that there will be problems and setbacks, but knowing also that nothing can stand in the way of your completing your plan if it is backed by persistence and determination.

Keep money in its proper place. It is a servant, nothing more. It is a tool with which you can live better and see more of the world around you. Money is necessary in your modern life. But you need only so much of it to live comfortably, securely, and well. Too much emphasis on money can reverse your whole picture and make you the servant and your money your master.

You do want to have money and the things it can buy, but you also must check up continually to make sure that you haven't lost the things that money cannot buy.

Three Financial Periods

Now let's look at your financial life. It will most likely be composed of three periods: the "Learning Period"; the "Earning Period"; and the "Yearning" or "Golden Period," depending on the decisions you make in your earning period.

Let's examine each of these financial periods.

3 Financial Periods

Age 1-25	25-65	65–?
LEARN	EARN	YEARN or GOLDEN

The Learning Period

I hope that you begin learning at birth and never cease to learn until you bid this world good-bye. The fact that you are reading this book indicates that you are. However, your formal learning period will probably last for your first twenty-five years, depending on your vocation.

If you are considering whether a college education is a good investment for yourself, your children, or your grandchildren, the answer is yes. It will cost between $15,000 and $50,000, depending on your choice of schools, vocation, and number of years before entering college. But the investment can yield a good return. Studies show that a college graduate earns $250,000 to $400,000 more during his life than does a person with only a high school diploma. Time, money, and effort invested in education increase the productivity of the individual. This investment in human capital is similar to an investment in capital equipment for a plant that increases productivity, which in turn yields an increase in profits. A college education can bring more than just financial rewards. The ability to think and to plan is stimulated in college. There are fewer divorces among college graduates. A college education can add a greatly enlarged dimension to life. And it is an asset that cannot be confiscated through taxation or other means.

There are many who want to believe that financial gains come by luck. I do not believe in luck. "Luck" comes when preparedness and opportunity get together. I have found that the more I place myself in the path of opportunity, the luckier I become. I have never learned a new tax law or mastered a new investment concept that I haven't had an opportunity to use advantageously immediately.

As I observe many around me, I am reminded of the man who stood in front of a wood burning stove and said, "Give me some heat and I'll give you some wood." But that's just not the nature of the wood burning stove. The wood must come first. The same is true of preparation, so do not skimp on this important ingredient. Put adequate wood in your burner, and it will yield the warmth of financial security.

However, never make the mistake of thinking that you can rest on your laurels of accumulated knowledge, for you are living in a dynamic world of change that makes it absolutely essential to obtain new information every day. I hope you did not end your education upon your graduation, but that yours was truly a commencement exercise whereupon you began your education.

The Earning Period

The second period of your financial life will be your "earning" period. This will probably last for around forty years, from age twenty-five to age sixty-five. This is when you apply the vocation that you have learned during the first period of your life.

Have you ever thought of how much money will come your way during those forty earning years, or have you just thought of your earnings as so much money a month? Add it up and you'll see that a tremendous amount of money will pass your way. Even if you never earn more than $525 a month, over a quarter of a million dollars will pass your way. If you earn $1,050 a month, over half a million dollars will pass your way. If you earn as much as $2,500 a month, over a million dollars will pass your way.

Monthly Income	10 Years	20 Years	30 Years	40 Years
$ 500	$ 60,000	$120,000	$ 180,000	$240,000
600	72,000	144,000	216,000	288,000
800	96,000	192,000	288,000	384,000
1,000	120,000	240,000	360,000	480,000
1,500	180,000	360,000	540,000	720,000
2,000	240,000	480,000	720,000	960,000
2,500	300,000	600,000	900,000	1,200,000
3,000	360,000	720,000	1,080,000	1,440,000

As you can see from the above chart, there is no question that a lot of money will come your way. What's the problem? It's how to keep some of it from passing through your fingers, isn't it?

. . . at only $2000 per month, $960,000 will pass through your hands during your earning years . . .

17

The Secret of Accumulation of Wealth

Let me share with you a very simple secret for the accumulation of wealth. The secret has only ten words in it and is so simple you will be tempted to discard it. But if you remember it and put it to use, it will be of great value to you for the remainder of your life. The secret is this: "A part of all I earn is mine to keep."

You may be tempted to say, "Everything I earn is mine to keep." It isn't so, is it? It belongs to the IRS, the baker, the butcher, the mortgage company, the church. If you were to place in a line, in the order of their importance to you, all those whom you wanted to receive a portion of your paycheck, would you place yourself at the head of the line? Is that where you have been putting yourself? If you are like so many others, you've put yourself at the end of the line, trying to save what is left over and finding that your ability to spend up to and beyond your income is utterly amazing. You must learn to pay yourself first or, if not first, at least along with the others.

If you were to save one-tenth of all you earned and did it for ten years, how much money would you have? A whole year's salary at one time, of course. And that's not all, for you would put this money to work, and before long you would have much more working for you.

The Yearning or Golden Years

The third period in your life will be your retirement years. These will be either your "yearning" years or your "golden" years, depending on the financial decisions you make during your "earning" years.

YEARNING   GOLDEN

If you are a male of age sixty-five, you will probably live to around seventy-nine years of age. If one of us females makes it to sixty-five, please be prepared to have us for a very long time. You can hardly kill off an old woman—we are sturdy! My oldest client is ninety-six years of age. Three years ago I got her to quit investing for growth!

Will this period of your life take care of itself? The answer is NO. The future belongs to those who prepare for it—and how tragically few are preparing!

Why, in a nation with a high per capita income and unparalleled prosperity, do 98 percent of our citizens reach sixty-five without having made adequate preparation for retiring in financial dignity?

Perhaps they—and you—have been lulled into a false sense of security by the cozy sound of the words Social Security. (Social Security, especially if you say it softly and slowly, does sound like a warm puppy.) You may find out all too soon that it should have been called "Social Insecurity." By that time it may be too late to alter your financial fate.

Actually, Social Security was never meant to provide you with financial independence. It was designed to prevent mass destitution. If you count on it at all, which I don't recommend, treat it as a very miniscule part of your financial plan, for the probability of it making a meaningful contribution to your retirement is slim.

It may surprise you to learn that when you reach the age to qualify for Social Security benefits, if your income from it and other sources is insufficient for you to live in financial dignity, making it necessary for

you to continue to work, you will forfeit all or most of your Social Security benefits over $6,000 (scheduled to go to $6,480) until you reach age seventy.

Today, 3.6 million of our citizens over sixty-five are caught in this financial trap and are forced to lose Social Security benefits; 1.1 million of these have reduced benefits; and 2.5 million are working but do not earn enough to lose benefits.

Most of them paid their hard-earned dollars into the system all of their working years. But they are disqualified from receiving benefits because these are not enough to keep body and soul together, for their average Social Security payment is only $385.51 per month.

If they had made provisions outside of Social Security, they could now be receiving unlimited income from capital in the form of dividends, rents, interest, and royalties and still be receiving their Social Security checks.

You may live a long time; yet longevity may be a mixed blessing. You may decide how long you will work, or it may be decided for you, but the decision of how long you will live is not in your hands.

Present-day medical science is getting so good at making us live longer that for every ten years we live, they add another four years to our life expectancy. Medical science may be adding years to your life, but it is still up to you to add some life to those years. Money is a necessity. It will not of itself bring you happiness—it will only give you options. However, I have yet to meet a person who found joy in poverty.

Never confuse piety and poverty. Until you are financially independent, you are an economic slave. Slavery does not bring the self-esteem each of us must possess. I believe our Maker wants us all to prosper and be in good health.

Have you ever considered what the difference is between an "old man" and an "elderly gentleman" in the eyes of the world? It's no other than income.

How Much Money Will You Need?

Since one of your objectives is to have sufficient funds to retire in financial dignity, you might ask how much will it take? I really don't know, but let's see if we can get a bit of a handle on the situation.

The amount of money you will need at retirement time will depend on the standard of living you wish to maintain, the number of years before you retire, the destruction inflation will have brought to the purchasing power of money, your ability and willingness to apply what you'll learn in this book to produce the maximum income and growth during retirement, and the number of years you will live.

To get some idea of the amount that may be required, let's begin

Table 1-1. Additional Income Needed (in Dollars)
at Retirement, with Various Inflation Rates

Years Until Retirement	5%	8%	10%	12%	15%
10	1.63	2.16	2.59	3.11	4.05
11	1.71	2.33	2.85	2.48	4.65
12	1.80	2.52	3.14	3.90	5.35
13	1.89	2.72	3.45	4.36	6.15
14	1.98	2.94	3.80	4.89	7.08
15	2.08	3.17	4.18	5.47	8.14
16	2.18	3.43	4.60	6.13	9.36
17	2.29	3.70	5.05	6.87	10.77
18	2.41	4.00	5.56	7.69	12.38
19	2.53	4.32	6.12	8.61	14.23
20	2.65	4.66	6.73	9.65	16.37
21	2.79	5.03	7.40	10.80	18.82
22	2.93	5.44	8.14	12.10	21.64
23	3.07	5.87	8.95	13.55	24.89
24	3.23	6.34	9.85	15.18	28.63
25	3.39	6.85	10.83	17.00	32.92
26	3.56	7.40	11.92	19.04	37.86
27	3.73	7.99	13.11	21.32	43.54
28	3.92	8.63	14.42	23.88	50.07
29	4.12	9.32	15.86	26.75	57.58
30	4.32	10.06	17.45	29.96	66.22
31	4.54	10.87	19.19	33.56	76.14
32	4.76	11.74	21.11	37.58	87.57
33	5.00	12.68	23.23	42.09	100.70
34	5.25	13.69	25.55	47.14	115.80
35	5.52	14.79	28.10	52.80	133.18

with what you would need if you were retiring today and then adjust your figures by what you think the future rate of inflation will be.

Table 1-1 shows rates of inflation from 5 to 15 percent. I cannot tell you what future inflation rates will be. They could subside with the change in mental attitude that is occurring across the nation—people are beginning to question the validity of trying to carry one another around on their backs. This is a judgment you must make for yourself. Table 1-1 can help you relate that judgment to dollars. Subtract your age from sixty-five to obtain the number of years before retirement (if this is the age at which you plan to retire). Read across the top and find the rate of inflation you think it is safe for you to assume. There you will find how many dollars it will take then to buy the same amount of groceries that a dollar buys today.

For example, assume that you would need $2,000 per month if you were retiring today, that you are age forty-five, that you plan to retire in twenty years at age sixty-five, and that you think the government can slow inflation to 5 percent. Go down the left-hand column to 20 and across four columns to 2.65, your adjustment factor. Now let's adjust: $2,000 x 2.65 = $5,300. This would be the amount you would need per month in twenty years to obtain the same housing, food, and clothing as you do with $2,000 today.

Inflation will probably not accommodate you by stopping when you retire, so you should plan for an additional amount to cover continued inflation.

How Much Capital Does This Require?

How much capital will it take to produce $5,300 per month?

Shall we use a 6 percent yield? If so, you will need $1,060,000 of capital ($5,300 x 200 = $1,060,000). At an 8 percent yield, you can reduce this amount to $795,000; at a 12 percent yield you can lower the amount to $530,000. That's a lot of capital. Before you become discouraged, remember that you have twenty years before you need it, and if you decide to use a portion of your principal each month during retirement, this amount can be reduced. There is nothing sacred about principal. The sacred thing is to make you and it come out together!

Incidentally, since my first book was published back in 1975, we have received thousands of calls asking why I multiplied the monthly income desired by 200 to obtain the amount of capital required. If you'll take 12 and divide by the rate of return and multiply your answer by the monthly amount, it will give you the amount of capital required to produce that monthly income. For example, 12 ÷ .06 = 200; $5,300 x 200 = $1,060,000, the capital needed to produce $5,300 per month at 6 percent. At 8 percent, you would multiply by 150 (12 ÷ .08).

Monthly Savings Needed

How much will you need to invest each month if you average 6 percent on your investment (see Table 1-2)? (Surely when you've completed this book you will be able to double that amount.)

As you can see, time is a powerful ally in accomplishing your goal. If your goal is $300,000 and you begin when you are twenty-five, you can reach it by saving $153 per month. If you wait until forty, you will need to save $429 per month.

If you put your money to work at 12 percent, and you must do that well, you can either reduce the amount you must invest by half; or better, you can increase your goal to $600,000.

Table 1-2. Monthly Savings Needed at 6% Interest
(Compounded Annually) to Attain Predetermined
Amount of Capital

			Desired Amount			
AGE NOW	YEARS TO RETIRE- MENT	MONTHS TO RETIRE- MENT	$200,000	$300,000	$500,000	$1,000,000
25	40	480	$ 102	$ 153	$ 255	$ 510
30	35	420	140	210	350	700
35	30	360	198	297	495	990
40	25	300	286	429	715	1430
45	20	240	426	639	1065	2130
50	15	180	674	1011	1685	3370
55	10	120	1192	1788	2980	5960

Time, Not Instant Pudding

Time can be a great ally in accomplishing your financial goal. Use it to your advantage, rather than trying to reach your goal fast, as tempting as that may be.

You will be tempted, for we live in an age of "instants." We drink instant coffee, eat instant pudding, spoon instant soup. Do not make the mistake of trying to carry this over to your money world. It takes time to accumulate a living estate. Many have difficulty accepting this fact of life. Many of our citizens have adopted an attitude of impatience, perhaps at the cost of serenity and physical and mental well-being. On the other hand, impatience to get things done deserves much of the credit for the achievements of Americans in building one of the wealthiest nations in the world.

Time is important. As a matter of fact, it is the first ingredient of my formula for financial independence.

Formula for Financial Independence

This is the formula that I have used over the years and that has been so valuable to me and my clients:

Time + Money + American free enterprise =
Opportunity to become financially independent

Let's take a good look at what effect time, the rate of return, and the amount of money you have to put to work will have in accomplishing your financial goal.

Time—The First Ingredient. If you are young and have only a small amount of money to invest, don't despair, for you possess one of the most important ingredients for financial independence—the ingredient of TIME. It doesn't take much money to compound to a tidy sum if you have time for it to grow. A savings of $30 per month started at age twenty-five is equivalent to $90 a month started at age thirty-five, $300 at age forty-five, and $1,275 at age fifty-five (as indicated in Figure 1-2, page 31).

Or, if we calculate the importance of time in reverse, a savings of $50 a month for ten years at 12 percent is less than $25 a month for fifteen years.

Perhaps you have a lump sum of $10,000. Let's look at the difference time makes in your results:

Years	At 12 Percent
10	$31,058
20	96,462
30	299,599
40	930,509

These figures point out the importance of starting as early as you can to reach your predetermined goal. I hope you are granted a large amount of this first ingredient, and that you learn early the importance of putting each day of it to maximum use.

Money—The Second Ingredient. This is an ingredient that you have every payday or that you have acquired through previous paydays of your own or your industrious and generous forefathers.

Your next challenge is to put this money to work for yourself as hard as you no doubt had to work to get it. To become financially independent, you must save and let your money grow. Unfortunately, I observe many people who save and let savings institutions grow, building magnificent skyscrapers that add impressively to our skyline.

Rate of Return

The rate of return that you receive on your funds will be determined by how skillfully you put your money to work under our free enterprise system.

You have looked at how important time is in the accomplishment of your goal; now let's introduce another important factor, the rate of return, and look at the difference an additional 5 percent can make:

$10,000 Lump Sum Invested at 10 Percent and 15 Percent

Years	At 10 Percent	At 15 Percent	Difference
10	$ 25,937	$ 40,455	$ 14,518
20	67,274	163,665	96,391
30	174,494	662,117	487,623
40	452,592	2,678,635	2,226,043

If we assume that you can invest $100 per month, your results would be:

$100 Per Month Invested at 10 Percent and 15 Percent

Years	Amount Invested	At 10 Percent	At 15 Percent	Difference
10	$ 12,000	$ 21,037	$ 28,018	$ 6,981
20	24,000	75,602	141,372	65,770
30	36,000	217,131	599,948	382,817
40	48,000	584,222	2,455,144	1,870,922

Don't Fight the Battle Alone. Are you amazed at the difference an additional 5 percent can make in your results?

At 10 percent you contributed $58,000 in forty years, and the savings institution contributed $978,814 from their profits by investing your money in American industry, real estate, and natural resources.

On the other hand, if you obtained 15 percent on your investment, you contributed $58,000, and you let American industry, real estate, and natural resources contribute $5,075,779 to your wealth, for a difference of $4,038,965.

It is not necessary to fight the battle alone if you will apply the information contained in this book so that American free enterprise can be of help to you.

The Eighth Wonder

One of the best ways to obtain a graphic picture of the importance of the rate of return is to study compound interest tables. Compound interest tables are fascinating. In my opinion, the "eighth wonder of the world" is not the Astrodome, but compound interest. Tables 1 through 6 in the Appendix show compound interest results and will be of immeasurable help to you in your financial programming. Don't yield to the temptation of saying, "Oh, I probably can't understand them," and flip casually by. Take a moment now to study them and you'll be surprised to find some real jewels of information. I'll help you apply the information so you won't have to go it alone.

Lump-Sum Investment

Appendix Table 1 will show you how much a $10,000 lump sum will grow over the years at varying rates of return. If you haven't yet saved $10,000, just keep dropping zeros until you reach your category. If you are fortunate enough to have $100,000, just add a zero.

For example, if you have $10,000 to invest for a goal that is twenty years away and you can average 12 percent on your money, you will have $96,462 when that time arrives, exclusive of taxes. If you have thirty years, that $10,000 will grow to $299,599; in forty years it will be $930,509.

Monthly Investment Results

Let's assume you do not have a lump sum, but can invest $1,200 a year, for an average of $100 per month.

If you average 12 percent over a twenty-year period, your results will be $96,838; in thirty years, $324,351; and in forty years, $1,030,970. As you can see, the secret of financial independence is not brilliance or luck, but the discipline to save a portion of all you earn and to put it to work aggressively (see Appendix Table 2).

Annual Investment Required

In the Appendix you'll find two other very interesting compound interest, or yield, tables. Table 3 enables you to determine how much you'll need to save per year to accomplish your predetermined goal. This table

27

is based on a $100,000 investment. Just multiply to adjust to your goal. For example, you've determined you'll need $500,000 when you retire in twenty years, and you think you can average a minimum of 12 percent on your investments. That means that you must save $6,195, or $516 per month, to accomplish your goal.

If you started thirty years before retirement, you could reduce this to $154 per month.

Lump Sum Required

Further, let's assume you would like to know what lump sum you would need to invest at various rates of return to equal a given amount at the end of a specified period (see Appendix Table 4).

Again, if you have twenty years before retirement and you can average 12 percent on your investments and desire $500,000, you will need to make a lump-sum investment of $51,835. To point out the importance of time, if you had started thirty years before you would only need a lump-sum investment of $16,700.

Three Things You Can Do With a Dollar

There are only three things you can do with a dollar—spend, loan, or own. If you decide to spend your dollars, I hope you've had a good time, but you have cut off our conversation. The only money that I can help you invest is the money you decide to keep. If you decide you are not going to spend it now, but are going to keep it to spend at a later date—not that you are never going to spend it, since that's just too cruel a thought—there are only two things you can do with a dollar: loan or own.

You may "loan" it to a savings institution, placing it in what is commonly called a "guaranteed" fixed position. We'll look at ways this can be done in a later chapter.

You may also place your dollars in a position so that you can "own." You may own shares of American industry, real estate, commodities, energy, cinema, precious metals, precious gems, rare stamps, art objects, antiques, and so on. We shall discuss the many ways that you can "own" throughout this book.

Let me now share with you the Rule of 72. It's a very simple one that you can use without elaborate compound interest tables.

The Rule of 72

I have a degree in economics and finance, yet I was never taught this rule in college. It's an extremely valuable rule and you'll find it very useful. The Rule of 72 gives you the answer to the question of how long it will take to double your money—to make $1 become $2—at various rates of return.

If you obtain 1 percent on your money, it will take 72 years for $1 to become $2. If you obtain 1.3 percent, it will take 55.4 years; if you obtain 6 percent, it will take 12 years; if you obtain 12 percent, it will take six years; at 18 percent, four years; and at 24 percent it takes three years (see Figure 1-1).

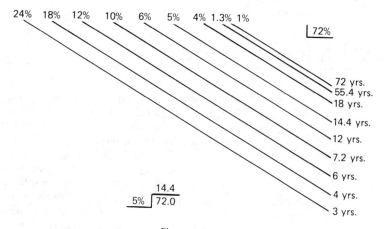

Figure 1-1.

When you came to 1.3 percent in the example above, did you say to yourself, "In these enlightened times no one would loan money at 1.3 percent." Unless you are one of the informed minority who have read and applied Chapter 13 of my last two books, you are probably loaning your money at 1.3 percent or less on the cash surrender value portion of your life insurance.

With the Rule of 72, you can see that at 6 percent $1,000 becomes:

$2,000 in 12 years
4,000 in 24 years
8,000 in 36 years

At 12 percent, $1,000 becomes:

$ 2,000 in 6 years
4,000 in 12 years
8,000 in 18 years
16,000 in 24 years
32,000 in 30 years
64,000 in 36 years

As you can see, it does make a difference how well you invest your money.

Which Rate Is Safer?

Which is the "safest" thing to do with your money—"loan" or "own"?

In the past, has it been safer to "loan" your money to a savings institution at 4–6 percent (or even for brief periods of time at 18 percent), or to "own" shares of American industry, real estate, and energy, with the hope of averaging 15 to 40 percent or higher? We shall take an in-depth look in this book at which way has truly been the "safest" long-term approach to money management. Suffice it to say here that if you have to wait eighteen years at 4 percent or twelve years at 6 percent for $1 to become $2, you have lost the fight, because inflation has more than doubled your cost of living—to say nothing of your loss through the tax bite.

Even at 10 percent your exercise has been similar to that of the little frog who was trying to hop out of the well. Every time he hopped up one foot, he slid back two. If you ignore change, inflation, and taxes, your money exercises may prove to parallel those of the little frog in the fairy tale of the frog and the princess, but without the kiss of the princess to miraculously make you an affluent prince.

"Stability" vs. "Safety"

In a later chapter I'll discuss the matter of stability and safety in more detail, but suffice it to say here that one of the most common mistakes made in the investment of money is that people confuse two very similar words that have very different meanings. These two words are "stability" and "safety." Stability is the return of the same number of dollars at a point of time in the future. "Safety" is the return of the same amount of food, clothing, and shelter. You can be "stable" and be far from "safe." This book is dedicated to helping you be a "safe" investor.

The $300,000 Estate

I encourage my clients to have as their minimum goal a $300,000 estate. I'll have to admit as soon as they reach it, I raise the ante. Your goal should be a minimum of this amount; and the younger you are, the higher your goal must be because inflation will continue to erode your purchasing power. A 6 percent yield on $300,000 is only $1,500 per month, and that's not easy street today. A 12 percent yield is $3,000.

Figure 1-2 is a handy chart showing how much you need to invest annually or monthly to reach a goal of $300,000 at 12 percent.

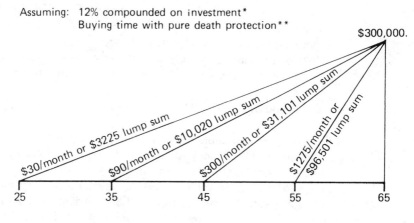

Assuming: 12% compounded on investment*
Buying time with pure death protection**

$300,000.

$30/month or $3225 lump sum
$90/month or $10,020 lump sum
$300/month or $31,101 lump sum
$1275/month or $96,501 lump sum

25   35   45   55   65

Investment for Living

Age	Monthly	or Lump Sum	Monthly Cost for $300,000 Death Insurance
25	$ 30	$ 3,225	$27
35	90	10,020	28
45	300	31,101	52
55	$1275	$96,501	113

*University of Michigan, Bureau of Business Research, Common Stocks & Yields.
**Based on rates of a leading insurance company.

Figure 1-2.

To all my good engineering friends, let me say that I am quite aware that money does not compound in a straight line, but in a curve. However, I have learned that only a few people can relate to a curve, but almost everyone can relate to a straight line— hence the straight lines. You will find a chart with the proper curves in Chapter 13, "Life Insurance—The Great National Consumer Dilemma. In that chapter, I also tell you how to buy time.

Pennies Become Millions

You may have seen this vivid illustration before, but let me repeat it, for it is such a graphic example of compounding.

Let's assume you had a choice of working thirty-five days with a pay of $1,000 per day or working for a penny the first day and doubling the amount each day for thirty-five days. Which job offer would you take?

If you took the first choice, at the end of the thirty-fifth day you would have received $35,000. What would you have received if you had made the second choice? You would have received $339,456,652.80. As you can see, one penny compounded at 100 percent per day produces over a third of a billion dollars by the thirty-fifth day. I realize this is an exaggerated example, but your rate of earnings is very important today in your quest for financial independence.

Get to know and fully comprehend interest rates, leverage, and how to compound your capital through good investments.

To Be More Specific

Perhaps your timetable does not fit into neat little five- and ten-year segments, and the money you have to invest is not in blocks of a $10,000 lump sum or $100 per month. In the Appendix you'll find tables that give you the necessary numbers to calculate a lump-sum investment at various rates of return from 2-1/2 to 15 percent and from one to fifty years. The first, Appendix Table 5, is titled "One Dollar Principal Compounded Annually." For example, if you have seventeen years before retirement and have $14,000 to put to work for that purpose, and you think you can average 12 percent, your factor would be 6.8660: $14,000 x 6.8660 = $96,124.

Let's assume that you can invest an additional $160 per month. Look at Appendix Table 6, titled "One Dollar Per Annum Compounded Annually." Go down the 12 percent column until you are opposite seventeen years and you will find your factor of 54.7497; $160 per month, times 12, times 54.7497 is $105,119.

So in seventeen years with a $10,000 lump-sum investment to which you have added $160 per month, you would have $201,243 (exclusive of taxes).

In 1748 Benjamin Franklin wrote, "Money is of a prolific, generating nature. Money can beget money, and its offspring can beget more." His was a definition and joyous explanation of the nature of money and one that can be of great value to you. Franklin's words "Money is of a prolific, generating nature" have a biblical ring to them, and well they may, because the Bible makes us aware that we are required to be good stewards of money.

You Are the Steward

I firmly believe that every dollar that comes your way comes there for a purpose. A portion of that dollar should be spent for the necessities of life, a portion for luxuries, a portion should be given away, and a portion should be invested for tomorrow's goods and services. I am also thoroughly convinced that you are the steward of every dollar that comes your way, and if you are not a good steward of that money it will be taken away from you.

The story of the talents in the Bible are as true today as they were when they were recorded. In Matthew 25:14-29 you will find these words:

> Again, the Kingdom of Heaven can be illustrated by the story of a man going into another country, who called together his servants and loaned them money to invest for him while he was gone. He gave $5,000 to one, $2,000 to another, and $1,000 to the last—dividing it in proportion to their abilities—and then left on his trip. The man who received the $5,000 began immediately to buy and sell with it and soon earned another $5,000. The man with $2,000 went right to work, too, and earned another $2,000.
>
> But the man who received the $1,000 dug a hole in the ground and hid the money for safekeeping. After a long time their master returned from his trip and called them to him to account for his money. The man to whom he had entrusted the $5,000 brought him $10,000.
>
> His master praised him for good work. "You have been faithful in handling this small amount," he told him, "so now I will give you many more responsibilities. Begin the joyous tasks I have assigned to you."
>
> Next came the man who had received $2,000, with the report, "Sir, you gave me $2,000 to use, and I have doubled it."

"Good work," his master said. "You are a good and faithful servant. You have been faithful over this small amount, so now I will give you much more."

Then the man with the $1,000 came and said, "Sir, I knew you were a hard man, and I was afraid you would rob me of what I earned, so I hid your money in the earth and here it is." But his master replied, "Wicked man! Lazy slave! Since you knew I would demand your profit, you should at least have put my money into the bank so I could have some interest. Take the money from this man and give it to the man with the $10,000. For the man who uses well what he is given shall be given more, and he shall have abundance. But from the man who is unfaithful, even what little responsibility he has shall be taken from him."

Let's analyze what the master considered good stewardship. He praised the two who "bought and sold" with the money entrusted to them, and gave them more. He severely reprimanded the one who dug a hole and buried the money, saying, "You should at least have put the money into the bank so I could have some interest." Note, however, that this was not what he recommended. Had the

Table 1-3. Interest Rates (Percent) Paid by Savings
and Loan Associations and by Banks

Year	Savings Accounts in Savings Associations	Deposits in Commercial Banks
1947	2.3%	0.9%
1948	2.3	0.9
1949	2.4	0.9
1950	2.5	0.9
1951	2.6	1.1
1952	2.7	1.2
1953	2.8	1.2
1954	2.9	1.3
1955	2.9	1.4
1956	3.0	1.6
1957	3.3	2.1
1958	3.38	2.21
1959	3.53	2.36
1960	3.86	2.56
1961	3.90	2.71
1962	4.08	3.18
1963	4.17	3.31
1964	4.19	3.42
1965	4.23	3.69
1966	4.45	4.04
1967	4.67	4.24
1968	4.68	4.48
1969	4.80	4.87
1970	5.06	4.95
1971	5.33	4.78
1972	5.40	4.65
1973	5.50	5.12
1974	5.55	5.15
1975	5.25	5.00
1976	5.25	5.00
1977	5.25	5.00
1978	5.50	5.25
1979	5.50	5.25
1980	5.50	5.25
1981	5.50	5.25

servant lived in the United States during the period when our banks paid 3 percent interest, in order for the money to have doubled, the master would have to have taken a twenty-four-year trip. Even if he had earned up to 5 percent, it would have taken 14.4 years. And at 8 percent it would have been a nine-year trip. By most standards, these would be very long trips.

Table 1-3 shows the rates paid by savings and loan associations and by banks from 1947 through 1981 for passbook savings.

Summary

In this first chapter you and I have come a long way toward determining what your goal must be to attain financial independence. We've had to cover a few charts and tables to give perspective to your challenge and to give you the assurance that you'll win the money game.

You've already seen that it will be necessary for you to save for the future so that you can fulfill your obligation to yourself, to your family, and to society. But you've also seen that you have all the requirements for financial independence and that you will not have to fight this battle alone. Your dollars can have fantastic earning power. Throughout the pages of this book you'll find your own personal powerpack.

Application

All the knowledge in the world will do you no good unless you apply it to your own particular set of circumstances. So at the end of each chapter I'll give you some questions to answer, some financial data to collect, and some specific tasks to perform.

May I suggest that you obtain a loose-leaf notebook and that you paste these words on the outside:

___(Your name)'s___ Progress Report Toward Financial Independence

Begin your notebook by listing the following questions and your answers to them. This notebook is for your eyes only, or for yours and those of your spouse if you are married, so be very honest with yourself and very specific.

1. What source or sources of income do I want to depend on at age 65?
2. How many years before I plan to retire?
3. What monthly income would I like to have if I were retiring today?
4. What inflation factor should I use?

5. How much will I need per month at retirement?
6. If I choose the guaranteed route, how much capital will be required?
7. What rate of growth on my investments is my minimum objective?
8. If I choose the variable route, how much capital will be required?
9. How much can I put to work today: (a) lump sum, (b) monthly?
10. What books am I going to read to assure myself that I'll develop and keep a winning attitude about money? You will find a recommended list in the Appendix.

Table 1. $10,000 Lump Sum at Varying Rates Compounded Annually—End of Year Values

	5th Yr.	10th Yr.	15th Yr.	20th Yr.	25th Yr.	30th Yr.	35th Yr.	40th Yr.
1%	10,510	11,046	11,609	12,201	12,824	13,478	14,166	14,888
2%	11,040	12,189	13,458	14,859	16,406	18,113	19,998	22,080
3%	11,592	13,439	15,579	18,061	20,937	24,272	28,138	32,620
4%	12,166	14,802	18,009	21,911	26,658	32,433	39,460	48,010
5%	12,762	16,288	20,789	26,532	33,863	43,219	55,160	70,399
6%	13,382	17,908	23,965	32,071	42,918	57,434	76,860	102,857
7%	14,025	19,671	27,590	38,696	54,274	76,122	106,765	149,744
8%	14,693	21,589	31,721	46,609	68,484	100,626	147,853	217,245
9%	15,386	23,673	36,424	56,044	86,230	132,676	204,139	314,094
10%	16,105	25,937	41,772	67,274	108,347	174,494	281,024	452,592
11%	16,850	28,394	47,845	80,623	135,854	228,922	385,748	650,008
12%	17,623	31,058	54,735	96,462	170,000	299,599	527,996	930,509
13%	18,424	33,945	62,542	115,230	212,305	391,158	720,685	1,327,815
14%	19,254	37,072	71,379	137,434	264,619	509,501	981,001	1,888,835
15%	20,113	40,455	81,370	163,665	329,189	662,117	1,331,755	2,678,635
16%	21,003	44,114	92,655	194,607	408,742	858,498	1,803,140	3,787,211
17%	21,924	48,068	105,387	231,055	506,578	1,110,646	2,435,034	5,338,687
18%	22,877	52,338	119,737	273,930	626,686	1,433,706	3,279,972	7,503,783
19%	23,863	56,946	135,895	324,294	773,880	1,846,753	4,407,006	10,516,675
20%	24,883	61,917	154,070	383,375	953,962	2,373,763	5,906,682	14,697,715
21%	25,937	67,274	174,494	452,592	1,173,908	3,044,816	7,897,469	20,484,002
22%	27,027	73,046	197,422	533,576	1,442,101	3,897,578	10,534,018	28,470,377
23%	28,153	79,259	223,139	628,206	1,768,592	4,979,128	14,017,769	39,464,304
24%	29,316	85,944	251,956	738,641	2,165,419	6,348,199	18,610,540	54,559,126
25%	30,517	93,132	284,217	867,361	2,646,698	8,077,935	24,651,903	75,231,638

Table 2. $1200 Per Year at Varying Rates Compounded Annually—End of Year Values

	5th Yr.	10th Yr.	15th Yr.	20th Yr.	25th Yr.	30th Yr.	35th Yr.	40th Yr.
1%	6,182	12,680	19,509	26,686	34,231	43,359	50,492	59,250
2%	6,369	13,402	21,168	29,739	39,205	49,654	61,192	73,932
3%	6,561	14,169	22,988	33,211	45,063	58,803	74,731	93,195
4%	6,760	14,983	24,990	37,162	51,974	69,993	91,917	118,592
5%	6,962	15,848	27,188	41,662	60,135	83,713	113,803	152,208
6%	7,170	16,766	29,607	46,791	69,787	100,562	141,745	196,857
7%	7,383	17,740	32,265	52,638	81,211	121,287	177,495	256,332
8%	7,603	18,774	35,188	59,307	94,744	146,815	223,322	335,737
9%	7,827	19,872	38,403	66,918	110,788	178,290	282,150	441,950
10%	8,059	21,037	41,940	75,602	129,818	217,131	357,752	584,222
11%	8,295	22,273	45,828	85,518	152,398	265,095	454,996	774,992
12%	8,538	23,586	50,103	96,838	179,200	324,351	581,355	1,030,970
13%	8,786	24,976	54,806	112,164	211,020	397,578	741,298	1,374,583
14%	9,043	26,454	59,976	124,521	248,799	488,084	948,807	1,835,890
15%	9,304	28,018	65,660	141,372	293,654	599,948	1,216,015	2,455,144
16%	9,572	29,679	71,910	160,609	346,905	726,194	1,560,032	3,286,173
17%	9,848	31,440	78,778	182,566	410,115	909,004	2,002,792	4,400,869
18%	10,130	33,306	86,326	207,625	485,126	1,119,982	2,572,378	5,895,109
19%	10,419	35,284	94,620	236,216	574,117	1,380,464	3,304,696	7,896,595
20%	10,716	37,380	103,730	268,831	679,652	1,701,909	4,245,610	10,575,154
21%	11,019	39,601	113,736	306,021	804,759	2,098,358	5,453,622	14,156,310
22%	11,330	41,954	124,722	348,416	952,998	2,587,006	7,003,256	18,939,087
23%	11,649	44,446	136,779	396,727	1,128,558	3,188,884	8,989,333	25,319,371
24%	11,976	47,085	150,013	451,758	1,336,360	3,929,683	11,532,334	33,820,458
25%	12,310	49,879	164,530	514,417	1,582,186	4,840,641	14,666,342	45,132,982

Table 3. Approximate Annual Investment Required to Equal $100,000 at the End of a Specified Period—Varying Rates

	5 Yrs.	10 Yrs.	15 Yrs.	20 Yrs.	25 Yrs.	30 Yrs.	35 Yrs.	40 Yrs.
1%	19,380	9,464	6,151	4,497	3,506	2,768	2,378	2,026
2%	18,841	8,954	5,669	4,036	3,061	2,417	1,961	1,624
3%	18,290	8,470	5,220	3,613	2,663	2,041	1,606	1,288
4%	17,751	8,009	4,802	3,229	2,309	1,714	1,306	1,011
5%	17,236	7,572	4,414	2,880	1,966	1,433	1,054	788.39
6%	16,736	7,157	4,053	2,565	1,720	1,193	846.59	609.58
7%	16,254	6,764	3,719	2,280	1,478	989.39	676.08	468.14
8%	15,783	6,392	3,410	2,024	1,267	817.36	537.34	357.42
9%	15,332	6,039	3,125	1,793	1,083	673.06	425.31	271.52
10%	14,890	5,704	2,861	1,587	924.37	552.66	335.43	205.40
11%	14,467	5,388	2,618	1,403	787.41	452.67	263.74	154.84
12%	14,055	5,088	2,395	1,239	669.64	369.97	206.41	116.40
13%	13,658	4,805	2,190	1,070	568.67	301.83	168.00	87.29
14%	13,270	4,536	2,001	963.69	482.32	245.86	126.47	65.36
15%	12,898	4,283	1,828	848.82	408.64	200.02	98.68	48.88
16%	12,537	4,043	1,669	747.16	345.92	165.25	76.92	36.52
17%	12,185	3,817	1,523	657.30	292.60	132.02	59.92	27.27
18%	11,846	3,603	1,390	577.97	247.36	107.14	46.65	20.36
19%	11,517	3,401	1,268	508.01	209.02	86.93	36.31	15.20
20%	11,198	3,210	1,157	446.38	176.56	70.51	28.26	11.35
21%	10,802	3,030	1,056	392.13	149.11	57.19	22.00	8.48
22%	10,591	2,860	962.14	344.42	125.92	46.39	17.13	6.34
23%	10,301	2,700	877.33	302.48	106.33	37.63	13.35	4.74
24%	10,020	2,549	799.93	265.63	89.80	30.53	10.41	3.55
25%	9,749	2,406	729.35	233.27	75.84	24.79	8.18	2.66

Table 4. Lump Sum Required to Equal $100,000 at the End of a Specified Period—Varying Rates

	5 Yrs.	10 Yrs.	15 Yrs.	20 Yrs.	25 Yrs.	30 Yrs.	35 Yrs.	40 Yrs.
1%	95,147	90,529	86,135	81,954	77,977	74,192	70,591	67,165
2%	90,573	82,348	74,301	67,297	60,953	55,207	50,003	45,289
3%	86,261	74,409	64,186	55,367	47,761	41,199	35,538	30,656
4%	82,193	67,556	55,526	45,639	37,512	30,832	25,341	20,829
5%	78,353	61,391	48,102	37,689	29,530	23,138	18,129	14,205
6%	74,726	55,839	41,727	31,180	23,300	17,411	13,011	9,722
7%	71,299	50,835	36,245	25,842	18,425	13,137	9,367	6,678
8%	68,058	46,319	31,524	21,455	14,602	9,938	6,763	4,603
9%	64,993	42,241	27,454	17,843	11,597	7,537	4,899	3,184
10%	62,092	38,554	23,940	14,864	9,230	5,731	3,558	2,209
11%	59,345	35,218	20,900	12,403	7,361	4,368	2,592	1,538
12%	56,743	32,197	18,270	10,367	5,882	3,340	1,894	1,075
13%	54,276	29,460	15,989	8,678	4,710	2,557	1,388	753.12
14%	51,937	26,974	14,010	7,276	3,780	1,963	1,019	529.43
15%	49,718	24,718	12,289	6,110	3,040	1,510	750.89	373.32
16%	47,611	22,683	10,792	5,139	2,447	1,165	554.59	264.05
17%	45,611	20,804	9,489	4,329	1,974	900.38	410.67	187.31
18%	43,711	19,107	8,352	3,651	1,596	697.49	304.88	133.27
19%	41,905	17,560	7,359	3,084	1,292	541.49	226.91	95.10
20%	40,188	16,151	6,491	2,610	1,048	421.27	169.30	68.04
21%	38,554	14,864	5,731	2,209	851.85	328.43	126.62	48.82
22%	37,000	13,690	5,065	1,874	693.43	256.57	94.93	35.12
23%	35,520	12,617	4,482	1,592	565.42	200.84	71.34	25.34
24%	34,112	11,635	3,969	1,354	461.80	157.52	53.72	18.33
25%	32,768	10,737	3,512	1,153	377.78	123.79	40.56	13.30

Table 5. One Dollar Principal Compounded Annually

End of Year	2½%	3%	5%	6%	8%	10%	12%	15%
1	$1.0250	$1.0300	$1.0500	$1.0600	$1.0800	$1.1000	$1.1200	1.1500
2	1.0506	1.0609	1.1025	1.1236	1.1664	1.2100	1.2544	1.3225
3	1.0769	1.0927	1.1576	1.1910	1.2597	1.3310	1.4049	1.5209
4	1.1038	1.1255	1.2155	1.2625	1.3605	1.4641	1.5735	1.7490
5	1.1314	1.1593	1.2763	1.3382	1.4693	1.6105	1.7623	2.0114
6	1.1597	1.1941	1.3401	1.4185	1.5869	1.7716	1.9738	2.3131
7	1.1887	1.2299	1.4071	1.5036	1.7138	1.9487	2.2107	2.6600
8	1.2184	1.2668	1.4775	1.5938	1.8509	2.1436	2.4760	3.0590
9	1.2489	1.3048	1.5513	1.6895	1.9990	2.3579	2.7731	3.5179
10	1.2801	1.3439	1.6289	1.7908	2.1589	2.5937	3.1058	4.0456
11	1.3121	1.3842	1.7103	1.8983	2.3316	2.8531	3.4785	4.6524
12	1.3449	1.4258	1.7959	2.0122	2.5182	3.1384	3.8960	5.3503
13	1.3785	1.4685	1.8856	2.1329	2.7196	3.4523	4.3635	6.1528
14	1.4130	1.5126	1.9799	2.2609	2.9372	3.7975	4.8871	7.0757
15	1.4483	1.5580	2.0789	2.3966	3.1722	4.1772	5.4736	8.1371
16	1.4845	1.6047	2.1829	2.5404	3.4259	4.5950	6.1304	9.3576
17	1.5216	1.6528	2.2920	2.6928	3.7000	5.0545	6.8660	10.7613
18	1.5597	1.7024	2.4066	2.8543	3.9960	5.5599	7.6900	12.3755
19	1.5987	1.7535	2.5270	3.0256	4.3157	6.1159	8.6128	14.2318
20	1.6386	1.8061	2.6533	3.2071	4.6610	6.7275	9.6463	16.3665
21	1.6796	1.8603	2.7860	3.3996	5.0338	7.4002	10.8038	18.8215
22	1.7216	1.9161	2.9253	3.6035	5.4365	8.1403	12.1003	21.6447
23	1.7646	1.9736	3.0715	3.8197	5.8715	8.9543	13.5523	24.8915
24	1.8087	2.0328	3.2251	4.0489	6.3412	9.8497	15.1786	28.6252
25	1.8539	2.0938	3.3864	4.2919	6.8485	10.8347	17.0001	32.9190

End of Year	2½%	3%	5%	6%	8%	10%	12%	15%
26	$ 1.9003	$ 2.1566	$ 3.5557	$ 4.5494	$ 7.3964	$ 11.9182	$ 19.0401	$ 37.8568
27	1.9478	2.2213	3.7335	4.8223	7.9881	13.1100	21.3249	43.5353
28	1.9965	2.2879	3.9201	5.1117	8.6271	14.4210	23.8839	50.0656
29	2.0464	2.3566	4.1161	5.4184	9.3173	15.8631	26.7499	57.5755
30	2.0976	2.4273	4.3219	5.7435	10.0627	17.4494	29.9599	66.2218
31	2.1500	2.5001	4.5380	6.0881	10.8677	19.1943	33.5551	76.1435
32	2.2038	2.5751	4.7649	6.4534	11.7371	21.1138	37.5817	87.5651
33	2.2589	2.6523	5.0032	6.8406	12.6760	23.2252	42.0915	100.6998
34	2.3153	2.7319	5.2533	7.2510	13.6901	25.5477	47.1425	115.8048
35	2.3732	2.8139	5.5160	7.6861	14.7853	28.1024	52.7996	133.1755
36	2.4325	2.8983	5.7918	8.1473	15.9682	30.9127	59.1356	153.1519
37	2.4933	2.9852	6.0814	8.6361	17.2456	34.0039	66.2318	176.1246
38	2.5557	3.0748	6.3855	9.1543	18.6253	37.4043	74.1797	202.5433
39	2.6196	3.1670	6.7048	9.7035	20.1153	41.1448	83.0812	232.9248
40	2.6851	3.2620	7.0400	10.2857	21.7245	45.2593	93.0510	267.8635
41	2.7522	3.3599	7.3920	10.9029	23.4625	49.7852	104.2171	308.0431
42	2.8210	3.4607	7.7616	11.5570	25.3395	54.7637	116.7231	354.2495
43	2.8915	3.5645	8.1497	12.2505	27.3666	60.2401	130.7299	407.3870
44	2.9638	3.6715	8.5572	12.9855	29.5560	66.2641	146.4175	468.4950
45	3.9379	3.7816	8.9850	13.7646	31.9204	72.8905	163.9876	538.7693
46	3.1139	3.8950	9.4343	14.5905	34.4741	80.1795	183.6661	619.5847
47	3.1917	4.0119	9.9060	15.4659	37.2320	88.1975	205.7061	712.5224
48	3.2715	4.1323	10.4013	16.3939	40.2106	97.0172	230.3908	819.4007
49	3.3533	4.2562	10.9213	17.3775	43.4274	106.7190	258.0377	942.3103
50	3.4371	4.3839	11.4674	18.4202	46.9016	117.3909	289.0022	1083.6574

Table 6. One Dollar Per Annum Compounded Annually

End of Year	3%	5%	6%	8%	10%	12%	15%
1	$ 1.0300	$ 1.0500	$ 1.0600	$ 1.0800	$ 1.1000	$ 1.1200	$ 1.1500
2	2.0909	2.1525	2.1836	2.2464	2.3100	2.3744	2.4725
3	3.1836	3.3101	3.3746	3.5061	3.6410	3.7793	3.9934
4	4.3091	4.5256	4.6371	4.8666	5.1051	5.3528	5.7424
5	5.4684	5.8019	5.9753	6.3359	6.7156	7.1152	7.7537
6	6.6625	7.1420	7.3938	7.9228	8.4872	9.0890	10.0668
7	7.8923	8.5491	8.8975	9.6366	10.4359	11.2297	12.7268
8	9.1591	10.0266	10.4913	11.4876	12.5795	13.7757	15.7858
9	10.4639	11.5779	12.1808	13.4866	14.3974	16.5487	19.3037
10	11.8078	13.2068	13.9716	15.6455	17.5312	19.6546	23.3493
11	13.1920	14.9171	15.8699	17.9771	20.3843	23.1331	28.0017
12	14.6178	16.7130	17.8821	20.4953	23.5227	27.0291	33.3519
13	16.0863	18.5986	20.0151	23.2149	26.9750	31.3926	39.5047
14	17.5989	20.5786	22.2760	26.1521	30.7725	36.2797	46.5804
15	19.1569	22.6575	24.6725	29.3243	34.9497	41.7533	54.7175
16	20.7616	24.8404	27.2129	32.7502	39.5447	47.8837	64.0751
17	22.4144	27.1324	29.9057	36.4502	44.5992	54.7497	74.8364
18	24.1169	29.5390	32.7600	40.4463	50.1591	62.4397	87.2118
19	25.8704	32.0660	35.7856	44.7620	56.2750	71.0524	101.4436
20	27.6765	34.7193	38.9927	49.4229	63.0025	80.6987	117.8101
21	29.5368	37.5052	42.3923	54.4568	70.4027	91.5026	136.6316
22	31.4529	40.4305	45.9958	59.8933	78.5430	103.6029	158.2764
23	33.4265	43.5020	49.8156	65.7648	87.4973	117.1552	183.1678
24	35.4593	46.7271	53.8645	72.1059	97.3471	132.3339	211.7930
25	37.5530	50.1135	58.1564	78.9544	108.1818	149.3339	244.7120

End of Year	3%	5%	6%	8%	10%	12%	15%
	$	$	$	$	$	$	$
26	39.7096	53.6691	62.7058	86.3508	120.0999	168.3740	282.5688
27	41.9309	57.4026	67.5281	94.3388	133.2099	189.6989	326.1041
28	44.2189	61.3227	72.6398	102.9659	147.6309	213.5828	376.1697
29	46.5754	65.4388	78.0582	112.2832	163.4940	240.3327	433.7451
30	49.0027	69.7608	83.8017	122.3459	180.9434	270.2926	499.9569
31	51.5028	74.2988	89.8898	133.2135	200.1378	303.8477	576.1005
32	54.0778	79.0638	96.3432	144.9506	221.2515	341.4294	663.6655
33	56.7302	84.0670	103.1838	157.6267	244.4767	383.5210	764.3654
34	59.4621	89.3203	110.4348	171.3168	270.0244	430.6635	880.1702
35	62.2759	94.8363	118.1209	186.1021	298.1268	483.4631	1013.3757
36	65.1742	100.6281	126.2681	202.0703	329.0395	542.5987	1166.4975
37	68.1594	106.7095	134.9042	219.3158	363.0434	608.8305	1342.6222
38	71.2342	113.0950	144.0585	237.9412	400.4478	683.0102	1545.1655
39	74.4013	119.7998	153.7620	258.0565	441.5926	766.0914	1778.0903
40	77.6633	126.8398	164.0477	279.7810	486.8518	859.1424	2045.9539
41	81.0232	134.2318	174.9505	303.2435	536.6370	963.3595	2353.9969
42	84.4839	141.9933	186.5076	328.5830	591.4007	1080.0826	2708.2465
43	88.0484	150.1430	198.7580	355.9496	651.6408	1210.8125	3115.6334
44	91.7199	158.7002	211.7435	385.5056	717.9048	1357.2300	3584.1285
45	95.5015	167.6852	225.5081	417.4261	790.7953	1521.2176	4122.8977
46	99.3965	177.1194	240.0986	451.9002	870.9749	1704.8838	4742.4824
47	103.4084	187.0254	255.5645	489.1322	959.1723	1910.5898	5455.0047
48	107.5406	197.4267	271.9584	529.3427	1056.1896	2140.9806	6274.4055
49	111.7969	208.3480	289.3359	572.7702	1162.9085	2399.0182	7216.7163
50	116.1808	219.8154	307.7561	619.6718	1280.2994	2688.0204	8300.3737

Addresses You'll Need to Know

American Birthright Trust Management
247 Royal Palm Way
Palm Beach, FL 33480
(305) 655-3481; also (800) 327-4508

American Funds Distributors, Inc.
333 South Hope Street
Los Angeles, CA 90071
(213) 486-9651

American General Capital Distributors
2777 Allen Parkway
Houston, TX 77019
(713) 526-8561; also (800) 231-3638

Anchor National Life Insurance Co.
2202 E. Camelback Rd.
Phoenix, AZ 85016
(602) 263-0363

Angeles Realty Corp.
10301 West Pico Blvd.
Los Angeles, CA 90064
(800) 421-4374

Arens's (Kurt) Gem Market Reporter
P.O. Box 39890
Phoenix, AZ 85069

The Balcor Company
The Balcor Building
10024 Skokie Boulevard
Skokie, IL 60066
(312) 677-2900

The Brennan Reports
William Brennan, Editor
P.O. Box 882
Valley Forge, PA 19482
(215) 783-0647

Brigham Young University
1222 SFLC
Provo, UT 84602
(801) 374-1211

College for Financial Planning
9725 East Hamptden Ave. Suite 200
Denver, CO 80231
(303) 755-7107

Consolidated Capital Equities Corp.
Suite 701, 333 Hegenberger Road
Oakland, CA 94621
(800) 227-1870; in California (800) 772-2443

Continental Trust Company
P.O. Box 367
Plano, TX 75074
(214) 422-1075

The Financial Planner Magazine
Forrest Wallace Cato, Editor
5775 Peachtree Dunwoody Rd., Suite 120-C
Atlanta, GA 30342
(404) 252-9600

Fireman's Fund American Life Insurance Company
1600 Los Gamos Road
San Rafael, CA 94911
(415) 492-6953

First Trust Corporation
Genro Building
444 Sherman St.
Denver, CO 80203
(800) 525-8188 or (303) 744-2944

Fox & Carskadon
2755 Campus Drive, Suite 300
San Mateo, CA 94403
(415) 574-3333

Institute of Certified Financial
Planners
9725 East Hamptden Ave, Suite 245
Denver, CO 80231
(303) 751-7600

Integrated Marketing, Inc.
660 Newport Center Dr., Suite 1420
Newport Beach, CA 92660
(714) 759-0451
National toll free (800) 854-3891
California toll free (800) 432-7203

International Association For
Financial Planners
5775 Peachtree Dunwoody Rd.,
Suite 120
Atlanta, GA 30342
(404) 252-9600

Investment Company Institute
1775 K Street, N.W.
Washington, D.C. 20006
(202) 293-7700

Investment Timing Services, Inc.
Boyce Plaza, Suite 120
1035 Boyce Road
Pittsburgh, PA 15241
(412) 257-0100

Jones Intercable, Inc.
880 Continental National Bank Bldg.
Englewood, CO 80110
(303) 761-3183

Life Insurance RX Corporation
P.O. Box O
Sausalito, CA 94965
(415) 332-2266

Lincoln Trust Company
P.O. Box 5831 T.A.
Denver, CO 80217
(303) 771-1900

Massachusetts Financial Services Company
200 Berkeley St.
Boston, MA 02116
(800) 343-2829; also (617) 423-3500

The Robert A. McNeil Corporation
2855 Campus Drive
San Mateo, CA 94403
(415) 572-0660; also (800) 227-6709

Money Dynamics Letter
Venita VanCaspel, Editor
Reston Publishing Company, Inc.
11480 Sunset Hills Road
Reston, Virginia 22090
(703) 437-8900

Morgan Petroleum Securities
Gary Stellow, President
700 Cass St.
Monterey, CA 93940
(408) 649-1111

National Tax Shelter Digest
Marilyn Passell Goldsmith, Editor
1720 Regal Row, Suite 242
Dallas, TX 75234
(214) 630-0684

New England Rare Coin Galleries
89 Devonshire Street
Boston, MA 02109
(800) 225-6794
In Massachusetts: (617) 227-8000

New York Institute of Finance
70 Pine Street, 2nd Floor
New York, NY 10005
(212) 344-2900

John Nuveen & Co., Inc.
61 Broadway
New York, NY 10006
(212) 668-9500

Oppenheimer Management Corporation
One New York Plaza
New York, NY 10004
(212) 825-8260

The Pioneer Group, Inc.
60 State Street
Boston, MA 02109
(617) 742-7825; also (800) 225-6292

Pioneer Western Corporation
P.O. Box 5068
Clearwater, FL 33518
(813) 585-6565, ext. 212

Public Storage
94 So. Los Robles
Pasadena, CA 91101
(213) 681-6731

Putnam Fund Distributors, Inc.
265 Franklin St.
Boston, MA 02110
(617) 423-4960, ext. 405-406

Research Institute Master Federal Tax
Manual
Mt. Kisco, NY 10549

Reston Publishing Company, Inc.
11480 Sunset Hills Road
Reston, VA 22090
(703) 437-8900

Success, The Magazine of Achievers
Dwight L. Chapin, Editor
401 N. Wabash Ave.
Chicago, ILL 60611
(312) 828-9100

U.S. Tangible Investment Corp.
Burnett Marus, President
7950 Elmbrook Dr., Suite 100
Dallas, TX 75247
(214) 631-1110; also (800) 527-9250

Universal Stamp Corp.
12 Richmond St. E, Suite 324
Toronto, Ontario, Canada M5C 1N1
(416) 862-1018

Van Caspel & Co., Incorporated
5051 Westheimer
1540 Post Oak Tower
Houston, TX 77056
(713) 621-9733

Waddell and Reed, Inc.
P. O. Box 1343
Kansas City, MO 64141
(816) 283-4021

Warren, Gorham & Lamont
210 South St.
Boston, MA 02111